Introduction: Why Start Early?

1. **The Power of Starting Young**
   Starting your financial journey before the age of 18 gives you an edge over the majority. While many people begin thinking about money in their twenties or thirties, teens have the unique advantage of time. Starting young means you have more time for learning, experimenting, and compounding your efforts. The earlier you begin, the faster you can build your wealth, allowing you to take full advantage of opportunities that may not be available later in life. With time on your side, you can learn, make mistakes, and recover quickly—something that's much harder to do once you have more responsibilities. In short, starting early maximizes your potential for financial success.

2. **How Time Is Your Greatest Asset**
One of the most powerful elements of wealth-building is time. As a teenager, you have something few adults can claim: decades of life ahead of you to grow your wealth. By investing early, even small amounts, you can see your money grow exponentially thanks to the magic of compound interest. The earlier you start saving, investing, or building a business, the more time you have for these efforts to multiply. This long runway allows you to make mistakes, learn from them, and still recover in time to achieve your financial goals. Your greatest asset is not

money—it's time, and starting early gives you more of it than you might think.

3. **Learning From Early Mistakes**
   Teens often make mistakes in their financial journeys, and that's okay. In fact, it's one of the best things you can do.

Making mistakes when you're young gives you the chance to recover with minimal consequences. Whether it's a bad investment, an unprofitable business venture, or spending money irresponsibly, these early lessons are invaluable. They teach resilience, problem-solving, and adaptability—skills that are crucial for long-term success. By learning early on how to deal with setbacks and failures, you set yourself up for a future where you can approach challenges with confidence and creativity.

4. **The Freedom to Take Risks in Your Teens**

Youth provides a rare opportunity to take calculated risks without the fear of losing everything. As a teenager, you likely don't have significant financial responsibilities—like a mortgage or a family to support—that would make taking risks more dangerous. Starting a business, trying new investment strategies, or experimenting with side hustles are all low-risk moves when you're young. This freedom to explore new ideas and pivot quickly is one of the most valuable aspects of starting early. The lessons learned from these risks—whether they result in success or failure—

can set the stage for bigger opportunities in the future.

Chapter 1: The Millionaire Mindset

5. The Psychology of Wealth: Mindset vs. Skills

Achieving financial success begins in the mind. While skills and strategies are essential, your mindset is the foundation for everything you do. A person with the right mindset can overcome challenges, maintain discipline, and stay focused on long-term goals. On the other hand, a person with a limiting mindset might sabotage their own progress, even with the best skills at their disposal. Cultivating a millionaire mindset involves believing in your ability to achieve greatness, understanding that success is a marathon, and remaining calm and focused in the face of adversity.

6. Overcoming Limiting Beliefs About Money

Many people are held back from financial success by deep-rooted beliefs about money, such as "I'll never be rich," or "Money doesn't grow on trees." These beliefs can stop you from taking the necessary actions to build wealth. To become a millionaire before 18, you must identify and challenge these limiting beliefs. Instead of seeing money as a scarce resource, you'll learn to view it as something that can be earned, invested, and multiplied. Recognizing and changing these thought patterns is crucial for building a prosperous future.

7. **Developing a Growth-Oriented Mindset**
A growth mindset is the belief that your abilities and intelligence can be developed over time with effort, learning, and persistence. This mindset is essential for anyone looking to build wealth because it allows you to embrace challenges, learn from criticism, and find inspiration in others' success. When you view every experience—good or bad—as an

opportunity for growth, you're more likely to take the necessary actions to succeed. Adopting a growth mindset will help you navigate the ups and downs of entrepreneurship and investing with a positive, can-do attitude.

8. **How to Build Discipline and Consistency**

Discipline and consistency are two of the most powerful tools in wealth-building. Without them, even the best strategies will fail. Developing discipline involves creating good habits, sticking to your plans even when things get tough, and making the necessary sacrifices to stay on track. Consistency is key to long-term success—whether it's saving a set amount each month, working on your skills daily, or making regular investments. By committing to these two principles, you'll be able to create a strong foundation for your financial journey.

9. **The Role of Resilience in Wealth-Building**

Resilience is the ability to bounce back from setbacks, challenges, and failures. On the road to becoming a millionaire, you'll inevitably face obstacles—whether it's a failed business idea, a bad investment, or unexpected expenses. Resilience allows you to learn from these setbacks without giving up. Instead of seeing failure as the end, you'll view it as a stepping stone toward future success. Building resilience means being able to persevere through tough times, keep a positive outlook, and maintain your long-term vision, no matter how many bumps you hit along the way.

10. Creating a Vision for Financial Success

Having a clear, compelling vision for your financial future is crucial for staying motivated and focused. Your vision should reflect your goals, values, and what financial freedom means to you. It's not just about accumulating wealth, but about what that wealth can bring—freedom, opportunities, security, and the ability to make a positive impact. By creating a detailed vision of what you want to achieve, you'll be able to maintain clarity and purpose, even when faced with distractions or difficulties. Your vision will keep you grounded and help you stay on track as you build your path to financial success.

11. Embracing Failure as Part of Success

Failure is not the opposite of success; it is an essential part of it. In fact, most successful people have failed more times than they can count. The key is to embrace failure as a learning experience rather than something to be feared. Every failure provides valuable insights and lessons that can be applied to future endeavors. If you can embrace failure and keep moving forward, it will fuel your growth and development, ultimately bringing you closer to your goal of becoming a millionaire before 18.

12. How to Cultivate a Problem-Solving Mindset

Being able to identify problems and come up with solutions is one of the most important skills you can develop on your path to financial success. A problem-solving mindset involves looking at challenges objectively, thinking critically, and coming up with creative solutions. Whether you're facing a business challenge, a financial issue, or a personal setback, this mindset allows you to approach problems with confidence and clarity. By developing problem-solving skills, you'll be able to navigate obstacles more easily and turn challenges into opportunities for growth.

13. The Importance of Self-Belief and Confidence

Self-belief and confidence are integral to achieving success, especially at a young age. Without these qualities, it can be difficult to take action or push through challenges. Believing in yourself allows you to take risks, try new things, and keep going even when things don't go as planned. Confidence doesn't mean you know everything or are perfect—it simply means you trust your ability to learn, adapt, and ultimately succeed. Cultivating self-belief and confidence will give you the courage to pursue your financial goals and the resilience to stay on track when challenges arise.

Chapter 2: Setting SMART Goals

14. **Understanding SMART Goals**
SMART goals are a powerful framework to transform abstract ideas into actionable objectives. SMART stands for Specific, Measurable, Achievable, Relevant, and Time-bound. The key to success is being specific about what you want to achieve, measurable so you can track your progress, and realistic enough to be possible given your resources. A SMART

goal should be relevant to your broader vision of wealth and have a clear deadline. This chapter helps you craft goals that are not only clear and actionable but also tailored to your personal aspirations, setting the foundation for long-term success.

15. Setting Short-Term and Long-Term Financial Goals

Setting both short-term and long-term financial goals is essential for maintaining focus and direction. Short-term goals might include saving a specific amount of money, starting a side hustle, or learning a new high-income skill, while long-term goals could involve building a business, purchasing an investment property, or achieving financial independence. This chapter emphasizes the importance of breaking down long-term goals into manageable steps, ensuring that you stay motivated and on track while you work toward your ultimate financial aspirations.

16. Tracking and Measuring Your Progress

Setting goals is just the first step—tracking your progress is what keeps you accountable. This chapter explores different methods of tracking your financial milestones, such as using spreadsheets, budgeting apps, or creating a personal financial dashboard. Measuring progress not only helps you stay on track but also provides motivation when you see the tangible results of your efforts. You'll learn how to adjust your goals as needed, ensuring that you're always moving toward the next milestone.

17. Adjusting Goals and Staying Adaptable

As you work toward your goals, you may encounter unforeseen circumstances, such as changes in income, market conditions, or personal situations. This chapter discusses the importance of staying adaptable and being willing to adjust your goals and strategies when necessary. By keeping an open mind and continuously reassessing your approach, you can ensure that you stay on course and make the best decisions for your financial future.

18. Creating a Vision Board for Financial Success

A vision board is a visual tool that helps you stay focused on your goals by displaying images, quotes, and reminders of your desired future. This chapter walks you through the process of creating a vision board that aligns with your financial objectives. A vision board serves as a constant reminder of your dreams, helping you visualize success and motivating you to work hard toward your financial goals. Whether physical or digital, this creative exercise helps turn abstract goals into clear visual representations of success.

Chapter 3: Learning High-Income Skills

19. **What Are High-Income Skills?**
High-income skills are specialized abilities that allow you to command high pay in the marketplace. Examples include coding, graphic design, digital marketing, sales, and copywriting. These are skills that can be monetized in a variety of industries and are often in high demand. In this chapter, you'll explore the concept of high-income skills and learn how to identify the skills that resonate with your

interests and strengths. Building such skills gives you the power to earn more money and create financial opportunities without relying on traditional employment.

20. How to Identify Your Strengths

Before you can begin mastering high-income skills, you need to identify your strengths and interests. This chapter walks you through a series of exercises to help you determine what you're naturally good at and what excites you. By focusing on skills that match your strengths, you'll increase the chances of long-term success and satisfaction. Whether you enjoy problem-solving, creativity, or analytical tasks, understanding your strengths helps you select the right high-income skills to develop.

21. Resources for Learning High-Income Skills

Learning high-income skills doesn't require enrolling in expensive university courses. With the rise of online learning platforms, you can now access high-quality, affordable resources to learn valuable skills. This chapter highlights platforms like Udemy, Coursera, LinkedIn Learning, and YouTube, offering a wealth of tutorials, courses, and certifications to help you master a wide range of skills. By committing to self-education and continuous learning, you can build expertise in high-demand areas that will set you apart in the job market.

22. The Importance of Building a Portfolio

A portfolio is a collection of your best work that showcases your skills to potential clients, employers, or investors. Whether you're a graphic designer, writer, developer, or digital marketer, having a professional portfolio is essential for demonstrating your abilities. This chapter explains how to create a strong portfolio, even if you're just starting out, and how to use it to attract clients or job opportunities. A well-organized portfolio acts as both a resume and a marketing tool, helping you stand out in competitive fields.

23. **Mastering the Art of Networking**
Networking is a crucial part of advancing in any field. Building a network of like-

minded individuals and mentors can help you discover new opportunities, gain insights into your industry, and expand your reach. This chapter provides practical tips on how to network effectively, both online and offline. Learn how to leverage LinkedIn, attend industry events, and engage with others in your niche to create meaningful connections that will help you grow personally and professionally.

Chapter 4: The Magic of Saving Early

24. The Power of Compound Interest

One of the most compelling reasons to start saving early is the power of compound interest. Compound interest allows you to earn interest not just on your initial deposit, but also on the interest that accrues over time. This chapter explains how compound interest works and why starting early can make a massive difference in how much you accumulate over the years. With examples and visual aids, you'll see how small, consistent savings can grow exponentially over time, leading to significant wealth.

25. **Paying Yourself First**

One of the most effective saving strategies is to pay yourself first. This means prioritizing saving and investing a portion of your income before you pay for any other expenses. This chapter teaches you how to automate your savings to ensure you consistently set aside money for your future, whether through retirement accounts, savings accounts, or investments. By building the habit of saving first, you eliminate the temptation to spend money on non-essential items and ensure that your financial future is secure.

26. Creating a Simple Budget

Budgeting is the cornerstone of financial success. This chapter breaks down how to create a simple budget that works for you. You'll learn how to categorize your income, track your expenses, and determine how much you should save each month. A budget helps you stay on track with your financial goals, ensures you live within your means, and allows you to prioritize saving and investing. Whether you're using pen and paper or an app, creating and sticking to a budget is an essential habit for anyone looking to build wealth.

27. Cutting Unnecessary Expenses

Building wealth isn't just about earning more money—it's also about spending less. In this chapter, you'll learn practical tips for cutting unnecessary expenses and optimizing your spending habits. Whether it's eliminating subscriptions you don't use, cooking at home instead of eating out, or finding cheaper alternatives for everyday items, small savings can add up over time. By reducing wasteful spending, you free up more money for savings, investments, and business opportunities.

28. Setting Up an Emergency Fund

An emergency fund is a crucial safety net for your financial security. This chapter explains the importance of setting aside money for unexpected expenses, such as medical bills, car repairs, or job loss. You'll learn how much money you should aim to save in your emergency fund and how to keep it easily accessible. Having an emergency fund ensures that you don't have to dip into your investments or go into debt when life throws you a curveball.

Chapter 5: Investing Basics for Teens

29. **Understanding the Stock Market**

    Investing in the stock market is one of the most effective ways to build wealth over time. This chapter introduces the basic principles of how the stock market works, including concepts like stocks, shares, dividends, and market indices. You'll also learn about the difference between individual stocks and index funds, and how to assess the risks and rewards associated with each. By understanding the fundamentals of the stock market, you'll be well-equipped to start investing as a teen.

30. Diversification: Spreading Risk Across Investments

Diversification is a strategy that helps protect your investments by spreading them across different assets, such as stocks, bonds, and real estate. This chapter explains why diversification is crucial to minimizing risk and maximizing returns. You'll learn how to build a diversified portfolio that balances risk and reward, ensuring that your investments are resilient against market fluctuations. By diversifying, you reduce the chances of losing everything if one investment performs poorly.

31. **The Importance of Long-Term Investing**

When it comes to investing, patience is key. This chapter highlights the benefits of long-term investing, where the goal is to hold investments for many years, allowing them to grow and appreciate in value. You'll learn why long-term investing is less risky than short-term trading and how compounding works best over extended periods. The chapter also introduces strategies like dollar-cost averaging, which can help you invest consistently, even with small amounts of money.

32. Risk Management in Investing

Every investment carries some level of risk, and understanding how to manage it is crucial for long-term success. This chapter walks you through the different types of risks involved in investing, including market risk, interest rate risk, and liquidity risk. You'll also learn strategies for managing risk, such as diversifying your portfolio, setting stop-loss orders, and staying informed about market trends. By understanding risk management, you can make more informed investment decisions and protect your wealth.

33. Where to Start: Investment Accounts for Teens

To start investing as a teen, you'll need an investment account. This chapter explains the different types of investment accounts available to minors, such as custodial accounts and brokerage accounts. You'll also learn about how to open and fund your first investment account, as well as what types of investments are best suited for beginners. Whether you're investing in stocks, mutual funds, or ETFs, this chapter provides the guidance you need to start building your portfolio early.

Chapter 6: E-Commerce and Dropshipping

34. What is E-Commerce and How Does It Work?

E-commerce refers to buying and selling products or services over the internet. In this chapter, you'll learn how e-commerce has revolutionized the way businesses operate and how you can tap into this trend as a teen entrepreneur. You'll understand the different types of e-commerce models—such as B2C (business to consumer), B2B (business to business), and C2C (consumer to consumer)—and how you can choose the best model for your business goals. This chapter will set the foundation for your journey into e-commerce and teach you the basics of starting an online store.

35. **Starting a Dropshipping Business**
Dropshipping is an e-commerce business model where you sell products without holding any inventory. This chapter dives deep into how dropshipping works and why it's an ideal business model for teens looking to get started with minimal upfront investment. You'll learn about finding reliable suppliers, creating a user-friendly online store, and using platforms like Shopify or WooCommerce to manage your business. Additionally, you'll explore marketing strategies to drive traffic to your store, such as social media ads and influencer partnerships.

36. **Finding Profitable Products to Sell**
Selecting the right products to sell is crucial to your success in e-commerce. This chapter covers the steps to identify profitable products, including conducting market research, analyzing trends on

platforms like Google Trends and Amazon, and using tools like Oberlo or AliExpress for dropshipping. You'll learn how to identify niche markets where demand is high but competition is low, and how to validate your product ideas before launching them. This chapter will ensure that you choose the right products to maximize your chances of success.

37. Building Your Brand

A strong brand helps you stand out in the crowded e-commerce market. This chapter will teach you how to develop a compelling brand identity, from creating a memorable name and logo to defining your brand's voice and values. You'll learn how to build trust with your audience, which is essential for generating repeat customers. Additionally, the chapter explores how to create an engaging website that reflects your brand, including tips on website design, product descriptions, and customer service practices that enhance user experience.

38. Driving Traffic and Converting Visitors into Customers

It's one thing to have an e-commerce store, but it's another to get people to visit and make purchases. In this chapter, you'll learn how to drive traffic to your online store using paid ads, search engine optimization (SEO), and social media marketing. The chapter also covers strategies for converting website visitors into paying customers, such as optimizing your checkout process, using email marketing to nurture leads, and offering promotions or discounts to encourage sales.

Chapter 7: Social Media Income

39. Monetizing Your Social Media Presence

Social media platforms like Instagram, YouTube, TikTok, and Twitter are no longer just for fun—they're powerful tools for generating income. In this chapter, you'll learn how to monetize your social media presence by building a personal brand, attracting followers, and engaging with your audience. You'll explore different income streams such as affiliate marketing, sponsored content, selling your own products, and more. By leveraging your social media accounts, you can create a passive income stream while growing your online influence.

40. Choosing the Right Social Media Platform for Your Niche

Each social media platform has its own strengths and attracts different demographics. This chapter helps you choose the best platform for your niche. For example, Instagram is great for visual products, YouTube is perfect for video content and tutorials, and TikTok offers a platform for creative and short-form content. You'll learn how to analyze your audience and pick the platform that aligns with your content style, whether it's fashion, gaming, lifestyle, or entrepreneurship.

41. **Building a Loyal and Engaged Audience**

Building a successful social media presence isn't just about numbers—it's about creating a loyal community that interacts with your content and trusts you. This chapter delves into the strategies for growing your followers organically, including tips for creating authentic content, posting consistently, and engaging with your audience through comments, live sessions, and stories. You'll also learn how to use analytics tools to track your performance and understand what resonates with your audience.

42. The Power of Influencer Marketing

Influencer marketing has become one of the most popular and effective ways to make money on social media. This chapter teaches you how to become an influencer in your niche and how to collaborate with brands to promote their products. You'll learn how to negotiate sponsorships, set your rates, and develop authentic partnerships with companies that align with your personal brand. You'll also explore the ethics of influencer marketing and how to maintain transparency with your followers.

43. Social Media Advertising for Income

Paid ads can significantly increase your visibility and revenue. This chapter explains how to use paid advertising on platforms like Facebook, Instagram, and TikTok to grow your business. You'll learn how to create targeted ads, track ad performance, and optimize your ad campaigns for maximum return on investment (ROI). Whether you're promoting products, services, or affiliate links, understanding how to run effective ad campaigns will help you monetize your social media more efficiently.

Chapter 8: Freelancing and Content Creation

44. **Getting Started with Freelancing**
    Freelancing offers flexibility, creativity, and the potential for high earnings, making it a great option for teens. This

chapter walks you through the process of becoming a freelancer, from selecting a niche to finding your first clients. You'll learn how to set up profiles on freelancing platforms like Fiverr, Upwork, and Freelancer, and how to craft compelling proposals that attract potential clients. Freelancing allows you to turn your skills into income, whether you're offering services like writing, graphic design, web development, or virtual assistance.

45. Building Your Freelance Portfolio

A strong portfolio is essential for attracting clients in the freelance world. This chapter focuses on how to create an impressive portfolio, even if you're just starting out. You'll learn how to showcase your work, gather testimonials, and build a professional website or online presence that highlights your services.

Additionally, you'll find tips on how to offer pro bono or discounted services to build your portfolio quickly while gaining valuable experience.

46. Managing Clients and Expectations

Freelancing is about more than just doing the work—it's also about managing clients and delivering great service. This chapter provides practical advice on how to communicate effectively with clients, set expectations upfront, and deliver high-quality work on time. You'll also learn how to handle difficult clients, navigate negotiations, and ensure that you're compensated fairly for your efforts. By managing client relationships well, you build a reputation that leads to repeat business and referrals.

47. Exploring Content Creation Opportunities

Content creation is another lucrative avenue for teens to generate income. Whether it's starting a blog, creating a YouTube channel, or podcasting, content creation allows you to express yourself creatively while monetizing your audience. In this chapter, you'll explore different types of content creation, such as writing, video, and audio, and how to turn these into income streams through ads, sponsorships, or selling your own products.

48. Time Management for Freelancers and Content Creators

As a freelancer or content creator, time management is crucial to balancing multiple projects, meeting deadlines, and maintaining a healthy work-life balance. This chapter teaches you how to organize your schedule, prioritize tasks, and stay productive while avoiding burnout. You'll also explore tools and apps that can help you manage your time more effectively, such as task managers, calendar apps, and project management platforms.

Chapter 9: Staying Motivated and Overcoming Challenges

49. Maintaining Focus and Consistency

Becoming a millionaire before 18 requires discipline and consistency. This chapter provides strategies to stay focused on your goals, even when faced with distractions, setbacks, or moments of doubt. You'll learn how to break down your goals into small, manageable tasks, create daily routines that support your success, and maintain momentum over time. Consistency is key to achieving long-term financial success, and this chapter helps you stay on track.

50. **Dealing with Failures and Setbacks**

Failures are a natural part of the entrepreneurial journey. This chapter discusses how to embrace failure as a learning opportunity and how to overcome setbacks with resilience. You'll learn how to turn failure into fuel for future success by analyzing what went wrong, making adjustments, and persevering. Understanding that failure is not the end but rather a stepping stone to success is crucial for long-term financial growth.

51. Building Mental Toughness and Resilience

Mental toughness is essential when faced with the challenges of entrepreneurship. In this chapter, you'll learn techniques for building mental resilience, such as developing a growth mindset, practicing mindfulness, and managing stress. These tools will help you push through difficult times and stay motivated, no matter how hard the journey gets.

52. Seeking Inspiration from Young Entrepreneurs

Sometimes, all you need is a little inspiration to reignite your passion. This chapter shares stories of young entrepreneurs who became millionaires before the age of 18, offering you real-life examples of what's possible. By learning about their struggles, successes, and the steps they took to achieve their goals, you'll find the motivation to keep pushing toward your own financial freedom.

53. Celebrating Small Wins

In the pursuit of big goals, it's easy to overlook small victories along the way. This chapter teaches you the importance of celebrating progress, no matter how small. Recognizing your achievements helps boost morale and keeps you motivated. You'll learn how to set milestones and reward yourself as you achieve them, reinforcing positive habits and fueling your drive to reach the ultimate goal of financial independence.

Chapter 10: Leveraging Your Network

54. Building a Strong Network at a Young Age

Networking isn't just for adults—it's an essential part of growing any business or career, even as a teenager. This chapter teaches you how to build and maintain valuable connections early on. You'll learn the importance of attending events (in-person or virtual), joining online communities, and reaching out to mentors who can offer guidance. Networking opens doors to new opportunities, partnerships, and collaborations that can accelerate your path to wealth.

55. How to Find Mentors Who Can Guide You

Mentorship is one of the fastest ways to

grow in any field. This chapter covers how to find mentors who align with your goals, how to approach them respectfully, and what you can learn from them. Mentors can provide you with advice, resources, and emotional support. This chapter will teach you how to seek mentorship in areas like business, investing, marketing, and more.

56. Collaborating with Like-Minded People

Successful entrepreneurs often work with people who share their vision and goals. This chapter explains how to collaborate effectively with other teens or adults who are also on the journey to financial success. Whether it's starting a business together or working on a project, collaboration can amplify your efforts and bring diverse perspectives that foster innovation.

57. Networking for Future Business Opportunities

In this chapter, you'll learn how to cultivate relationships that will be useful in your entrepreneurial career. Networking isn't just about finding mentors or collaborators—it's about positioning yourself for future business ventures, partnerships, and investment opportunities. Whether you're networking with local business owners, influencers, or even classmates, these connections can prove invaluable later on.

Chapter 11: Entrepreneurship Skills

58. The Essentials of Starting a Business at a Young Age

Entrepreneurship is a key pathway to becoming a millionaire, and starting a business as a teen can provide invaluable experience. This chapter covers the basic steps to take when starting a business: from brainstorming ideas to registering your business, creating a business plan, and managing finances. You'll also learn about how to validate your business ideas, build a customer base, and launch your products or services effectively.

59. Developing Problem-Solving Skills

Entrepreneurs are excellent problem-solvers. In this chapter, you'll learn how to develop creative thinking and problem-solving skills. Whether it's solving a customer issue or finding a way to make your business more efficient, problem-solving is a key skill for success. This chapter provides practical techniques for identifying problems, coming up with innovative solutions, and testing them in real-world scenarios.

60. Understanding Supply and Demand

Supply and demand are fundamental concepts in any market. This chapter will explain how to assess market needs and create products or services that meet those needs. You'll learn how to conduct market research to identify gaps in the market and how to price your product or service to maximize both value and profit. Understanding supply and demand will help you make more informed decisions in your business ventures.

61. Marketing 101 for Young Entrepreneurs

Marketing is essential to growing any business, but it can be overwhelming. This chapter breaks down marketing strategies for young entrepreneurs, focusing on low-cost or free marketing tactics such as word-of-mouth, social media promotion, and influencer partnerships. You'll also learn how to create a marketing plan that aligns with your business goals, how to track success, and how to adapt your strategy over time.

62. Scaling Your Business: Taking It to the Next Level

Once your business is off the ground, it's time to scale. This chapter teaches you the steps to take your business to the next level. You'll explore strategies for increasing production, reaching new customers, and expanding your marketing efforts. Scaling requires strategic planning, investment, and a focus on growth. This chapter will help you identify when it's time to scale and how to do it effectively.

Chapter 12: Personal Finance Mastery

63. Creating a Personal Budget

Managing your personal finances is just as important as managing your business finances. This chapter will show you how to create a simple but effective personal budget, track your expenses, and prioritize savings. You'll learn how to create financial goals, set up automatic savings, and ensure that you're consistently living within your means, even as your income grows.

64. Understanding Credit and Debt

Credit is an essential part of your financial life, but it must be managed responsibly. This chapter explains how credit works, how to build a good credit score, and why having access to credit can help you in the future. You'll also learn the importance of avoiding high-interest debt, especially consumer debt, and how to use credit cards wisely to build credit without falling into financial trouble.

65. The Power of Compound Interest

One of the most powerful tools for wealth-building is compound interest. This chapter explores how compound interest works, how you can take advantage of it to grow your savings and investments, and why starting early is critical. You'll learn how compound interest impacts everything from savings accounts to investment returns, and how to maximize your earnings over time by investing early.

66. **Managing Taxes and Legal Issues**
Understanding taxes and the legalities of business ownership is crucial. This

chapter will explain the basics of tax planning for teens, how to keep track of your earnings, and what you need to know about reporting your income. You'll also learn about legal considerations, such as contracts, intellectual property, and licenses, which are important when running a business or investing in assets.

67. Financial Independence: Building Wealth that Lasts

Financial independence is the ultimate goal of any wealth-building strategy. This chapter shows you how to take control of your finances, build assets, and create multiple income streams so that you don't rely on a traditional job for income. It discusses the importance of long-term planning, creating passive income, and setting yourself up for a life where money works for you rather than the other way around.

Chapter 13: Advanced Wealth-Building Strategies

68. **The Power of Real Estate Investment**
    Real estate is a tried-and-true wealth-building tool. This chapter introduces the basics of real estate investing for teens, explaining how to start with little capital, whether through house hacking, rental

properties, or REITs (Real Estate Investment Trusts). You'll learn the key concepts of real estate investing, such as cash flow, property appreciation, and the risks involved, helping you understand how real estate can fit into your overall wealth-building strategy.

69. Building Passive Income Streams

Building passive income is key to achieving financial freedom. This chapter explores different ways to generate passive income, such as through investments, rental properties, affiliate marketing, digital products, and more. You'll learn how to create systems that generate money while you sleep, helping you earn without having to actively work for every dollar.

70. Creating a Portfolio of Investments

This chapter dives deep into the importance of having a diversified portfolio that includes stocks, bonds, real estate, and other assets. You'll learn how to balance risk and reward, choose investments that align with your goals, and keep track of your portfolio's performance. Building a strong investment portfolio early on can help you build wealth over time and achieve financial independence faster.

71. For those who are ready to take their wealth-building to the next level, this chapter introduces the world of venture capital (VC) and angel investing. It explains how to get started **Venture Capital and Angel Investing** with investing in startups, the risks and rewards of early-stage investments, and

how you can use your wealth to support innovative entrepreneurs. You'll learn how to research potential investments and become a successful investor in high-growth companies.

72. Philanthropy: Giving Back While Growing Wealth

Becoming a millionaire is not just about accumulating wealth—it's also about how you use that wealth. This chapter explores the concept of philanthropy and how giving back can be part of your wealth-building journey. You'll learn how to start a charitable foundation, donate to causes you care about, and use your financial success to make a positive impact on the world.

www.ingramcontent.com/pod-product-compliance
Lightning Source LLC
Chambersburg PA
CBHW050326230526
45471CB00005B/2367